T0332142

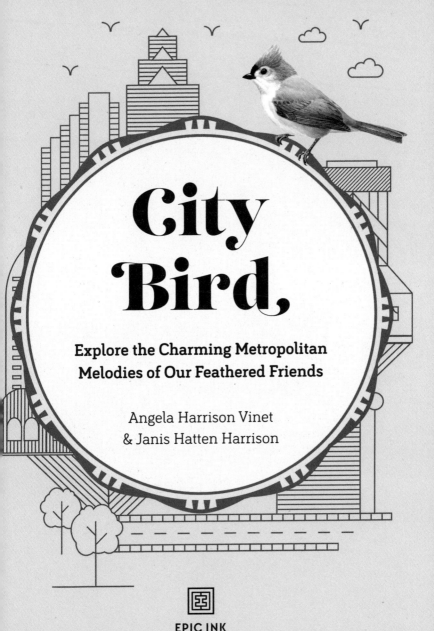

City Bird

Explore the Charming Metropolitan Melodies of Our Feathered Friends

Angela Harrison Vinet
& Janis Hatten Harrison

EPIC INK

First published in 2024 by Epic Ink, an imprint of The Quarto Group,
142 West 36th Street, 4th Floor, New York, NY 10018, USA
(212) 779-4972 • www.Quarto.com

Epic Ink titles are also available at discount for retail, wholesale, promotional, and bulk purchase. For details contact the Special Sales Manager by email at specialsales@quarto.com or by mail at The Quarto Group, Attn: Special Sales Manager, 100 Cummings Center Suite 265D, Beverly, MA 01915 USA.

10 9 8 7 6 5 4 3 2 1

ISBN: 978-0-76038-767-2

Digital edition published in 2024
eISBN: 978-0-76038-768-9

Library of Congress Cataloging-in-Publication Data

Names: Vinet, Angela Harrison, author. | Harrison, Janis Hatten, author.
Title: City bird : explore the charming metropolitan melodies of our
   feathered friends / Angela Harrison Vinet and Janis Hatten Harrison.
Description: New York, NY : Epic Ink, an imprint of the Quarto Group, 2024.
   | Summary: "City Bird is a lighthearted and humorous yet scientifically
   informed field guide to the birds of urban North America"-- Provided by publisher.
Identifiers: LCCN 2024006007 (print) | LCCN 2024006008 (ebook) | ISBN
   9780760387672 (hardcover) | ISBN 9780760387689 (ebook)
Subjects: LCSH: Bird watching--North America--Humor. | Urban animals--North
   America--Identification. | Birds--North America--Identification.
Classification: LCC QL681 .V56 2024 (print) | LCC QL681 (ebook) | DDC
   598.097/091732--dc23/eng/20240310
LC record available at https://lccn.loc.gov/2024006007
LC ebook record available at https://lccn.loc.gov/2024006008

Group Publisher: Rage Kindelsperger
Editorial Director: Lori Burke
Creative Director: Laura Drew
Managing Editor: Cara Donaldson
Editor: Katie McGuire
Cover Design: Scott Richardson
Cover Illustration: Hannah George
Interior Design: Evelin Kasikov

Interior illustrations by David Nurney, Diane Pierce, H. Douglas Pratt, and John Sill unless otherwise noted.
Page 22: Image courtesy National Gallery of Art; Page 40: © NPL - DeA Picture Library / Bridgeman Images;
Page 54: Histoire naturelle des oiseaux-mouches, ou, Colibris; Page 66: Biodiversity Heritage Library; Page
72, 78, 104: The New York Public Library

Printed in China

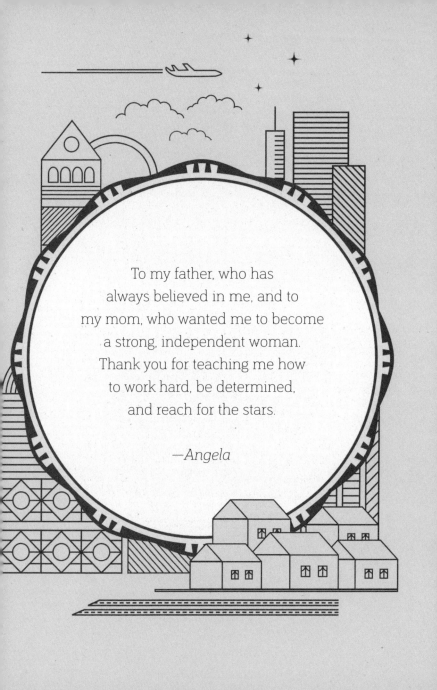

To my father, who has
always believed in me, and to
my mom, who wanted me to become
a strong, independent woman.
Thank you for teaching me how
to work hard, be determined,
and reach for the stars.

—Angela

Welcome to the Concrete Jungle
6

I'm Birdin' Here!
8

Your Flighty City Neighbors
13

Out on the Town
114

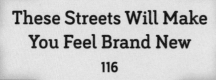

These Streets Will Make You Feel Brand New
116

Walking the Walk
118

Be a Part of It
122

Women of Letters
127

Top of the Heap
128

Welcome to the Concrete Jungle

Life in the city moves fast. While the allure of bright lights and a hurried pace keeps people gravitating toward city life, there is a need for balance—to take time to relax and recoup, away from life in the fast lane.

• — • • ● • • —

Birding offers much-needed respite in a busy world by being not only easy on the budget but also time. People in the city can bird during a lunch break, bird while on a date, or simply bird from the comfort of their own apartment. Do you have a window? A balcony? A fire escape? Then you're halfway there.

Birds *do* frequent the city. Some of our feathered friends find life delightful in the hustle and bustle of cityscapes, using manmade structures to launch into new spaces where they can adapt and thrive. This book is intended to help city slickers identify common birds found in their surroundings, while learning a little about bird habits and lifestyles.

I'm Birdin' Here!

Birding Tips for the Big City

Here are a few tips and tricks to get you started on your urban birding.

1 **It's always more fun to bird with a group.**
Birding alone has its advantages, but learning from others adds valuable knowledge and experience while in the field. Birding experts can offer the tricks of the trade that only come with life experience, passing on information to newer birders. You will learn more in one day with an expert birder than you can from reading 50 books. To find your flock, do an internet search for birding groups in your city.

2 **Invest in a good pair of binoculars.** Get the best pair you can afford. You don't need Swarovski binoculars—there are many excellent budget-friendly options! Some are lightweight, pocket-sized, and portable, which is all you really need in the field. Bird a while before you invest in expensive equipment.

3 **Find a window and take a seat.** There are birds all over any city. Armed with your binoculars and field guild, sitting still and watching will yield great birding rewards.

4 **Get a good birding book or app to help identify birds.** Your book of choice will be your birding lifeline. This resource will tell you about the feathering patterns, habits, feeding preferences, and habitat of birds. A phone app is even easier for a quick reference when in the field.

5 **Find green space; the birds will be there.** Bring your field guide, binoculars, water, and a snack. Use a chair or blanket to sit and observe what birds frequent the space. Birds love to come to water, so sitting in a green space by a river or pond means a more likely chance of seeing a bigger assortment of birds.

6 **Put out a feeder or a small bird bath wherever you can—in your yard, if you have one, or on your balcony, windowsill, or fire escape.** Add some plants, water, and perhaps a Hummingbird feeder and prepare to be shocked at what birds are nearby. If you build the space, they will come. Just make sure your seed feeder is permitted by the landlord or HOA, as it can make a mess. Another option is a hull-less type of food. Just feed those birds!

7 **Research birder hot spots.** Cornell Lab has a great site for this purpose. You can also check out live feeds of birds on the internet, like eagle cams or nest cams. Zoos and other conservancy organizations sometimes offer them to educate the public.

8 **Speaking of—try the zoo!** Surprisingly, native birds flock to zoos. Zoos offer all the important things birds are looking for: safety in the form of shelter, food from leftovers spilled by other animals, and water. They will be there if you start looking for them.

9 **Rooftops are a great birdwatching space.** Flat rooftops are an especially wonderful spot because several types of City Bird will make nests on them. You can observe the birds without interference by sitting quietly in a chair a safe distance from a nesting site.

10 **Start a list.** Every birder has a birding list with an active bird count. The more proficient a birder you are, the higher your number. (And you can keep track using the handy journaling pages at the back of this very book—see page 122.)

Your
Flighty City
Neighbors

···• Masters of Industry •···

If you're wandering a city park and notice a tree dotted with acorns drilled into the bark, there is an Acorn Woodpecker nearby. And where you find one Acorn Woodpecker, you'll find an entire group. These busy City Birds have remarkable coloring patterns around their face, though their pièce de resistance is their signature red head. So serious are these birds about their acorn cache, they leave guards to keep the precious nuts safe. They're also serious about their complex social hierarchy. The Acorn Woodpecker will often have younger birds helping out with their siblings and around the house for several years. This works well for their granary tree, as they add new holes every year in which to keep their precious acorns. Acorn Woodpeckers help raise several broods of young at once, putting all the family eggs in one basket.

···• Fast-Paced with a Pretty Face •···

The American Kestrel will have the hearts of birders and mice skipping beats. Though they're the smallest of the Falcon group, what Kestrels lack in size they make up for in speed and accuracy. This City Bird hunts unsuspecting ground prey while patiently perched high above all our heads. Roughly the same size as larger songbirds, the American Kestrel is small enough to be at the mercy of the wind, often tossed around like a leaf in a large gust. With decoy eye feathers in the back of its head, the American Kestrel eludes predators by keeping them guessing as to which way they are looking. These birds easily make their homes in bird-made or human-made cavities. Search telephone wires and light poles for a glimpse of the rusty reds, blues, and grays of the Kestrel, as they love a high perch to search for small mammals, reptiles, birds, and insects.

···• Diamond in the Rough •···

Hummingbirds are a delight to watch from any stoop or balcony, and can be enticed to visit with a simple feeder syrup of sugar water. The most common hummer, Anna's Hummingbird can be found on America's West Coast and is a dazzling little bird of emerald green, with a pink iridescent hood that shifts to black when not shimmering in the sunlight. Human activity has helped Anna's Hummingbird, with the planting of fruit trees all along the West Coast giving them food sources much closer to home. The dazzling feats these City Birds put on during courtship season make for a fun show. The male will high-dive, allowing the wind to create tail sounds, which brings the girls in. Once the ladies are watching, he'll make sure to position himself in the best lighting possible to show off his good looks. It's no wonder a flock of Anna's Hummingbirds is called a glittering!

···· Fly, Eagles, Fly ····

As America's great symbol of freedom, strength, and fierceness, the Bald Eagle serves the country well. Indigenous peoples across North America also held this bird in high regard. The US Fish and Wildlife Service offers a National Eagle Repository for Native Americans to continue to have access to Eagle feathers and other items for ceremonies without harming the species. Usually identified by their distinctive, brilliant-white head feathers, this City Bird fishes for its supper. The Bald Eagle is also a carrion eater, which adds to the fierceness of its image—it will eat you, dead or alive. When they fly with their talons out, spectators know this bird means business, whether it's in the air or on a football field in a major East Coast city on a Sunday. Look for Bald Eagle nests at the very top of the trees, as they are quite grand and hard to miss. The birds add to the same nest year after year for their fledglings to fly from. Urban life suits the Bald Eagle because they easily adapt to city living and don't mind their human neighbors. Always soaring high, the Bald Eagle is a bird of distinction commanding respect from all creatures great and small.

···• Out of the Rat Race ···•

Native to the western parts of North America, the Band-tailed Pigeon is as peaceful as they come. The soft blues and grays of their plumage reflect their soft personality. No pushing at the dinner table, no one squawking over the handouts—this City Bird is gentile and kind amongst friends. Hanging out in tall trees, flocks of Band-tailed Pigeons enjoy life in the slower lanes, feeding on seeds and fruits found in bushes and on the trees. Meandering along the outskirts of the city closer to the woods, the Pigeons will travel far from their nests to find their favorite foods. When searching for these Western City Birds, look for the gray body with a white band against the soft gray on the back of their neck. When they're in flight, you can catch a glimpse of the banded tail that gives them their name. A relaxed lifestyle pays off for longevity in the wild: Band-tailed Pigeons can live for upwards of 20 years.

King of the Punks

Daring feats of flight packing a sword-fighting punch? You must've spotted the Belted Kingfisher. The mohawk atop the Belted Kingfisher's head makes it clear this is a feisty little fisher, and their deadly accuracy gives them that majestic "king" status. The Kingfisher stealthily hunts prey in any fish-filled body of water, including poaching fish from backyard ponds. Male Kingfishers sword-fight during mating season to attract females and precision strikes with their beaks earn them top marks (and aquatic meals). The Belted Kingfisher burrows into the banks along their hunting grounds. This is where humans have assisted with their habitat expansion. As humans build earthen banks for roadways or bridges, the embankments serve as perfect City Bird homes. Inspect such sites for pellets of regurgitated scales or exoskeletons for a sure sign that a Belted Kingfisher calls the space home.

···· Hippies at Heart ····

Life is not a walk in the park for the Bewick's Wren. From the time this City Bird is but an egg in the nest, the Bewick's Wren serves as food for others. The lucky survivors become adorable adults, busy raising their brood, flicking their tails, and catching spiders. Identifying this bird is easy enough—just look for a hyper bird with white racing stripes on its head around brush piles. This bird and its cousin, the House Wren, compete for resources, and the House Wren fights dirty: they'll remove the Bewick's Wren's eggs from their nest. Once partnered up, the Bewick's Wren maintains a monogamous relationship, hardly leaving each other's sides as they take trips to the natural food store and keep an eye on the nestlings. The close bonds these birds form bleed into the males' songs as well. Like kids growing up in a supportive neighborhood, young males will learn their fathers' songs, as well as those of other influential males in the region.

BLACK-BILLED MAGPIE

··· Plenty to Say ···

Like a discourteous dinner guest, the Black-billed Magpie is always dressed to impress, but its manners leave something to be desired. From a distance, the Black-billed Magpie appears to have black and white plumage, but in the sun these feathers shine blue and green. It's astonishing how beautiful these City Birds are—until they speak. Their noisy squawks grate on the nerves of even the most seasoned city-dweller. Black-billed Magpies also have a tail that is just as long as their whole body, so they're never without their formal attire, even as they feed on carrion, their favorite dish. Look for these birds around roadkill, or around mammals with pests, because these Magpies can pick an animal clean of ticks faster than someone who slept through their alarm running to catch the train. Stories of Magpies dot American history books, with these birds stealing scraps from hunting parties hundreds of years ago. Showing little fear of humans, these birds have thrived around human development, adapting easily to city environments while also benefitting the ecosystem.

BLACK-CROWNED NIGHT HERON

···• Is This Fish Fresh? •···

Building stick nests over their aquatic hunting grounds, the Black-crowned Night Heron can be found near bodies of both salt- and freshwater within the city limits—as long as there are fish. Like their other Heron relatives, this bird utilizes its legs to hunt in hard-to-reach spaces, dining on anything from crawfish and small fish to voles and moles. Hunting at dawn or dusk, this bird is a fisherman and patient enough to catch its daily limit. And while the Black-crowned Night Heron lives amongst its relatives in a colony, they also enjoy the company of other water birds. Distinctive in feathering patterns, the sharp contrast of whites and grays along a shoreline should make them pretty easy to spot, but the dead giveaway is their ruby red eyes.

BLACK PHOEBE

···• Little Tyrant •···

Perched searching for insects, the Black Phoebe is quite common along the western coast of North America, often dining on a bug charcuterie found in people's backyards. It's best to search for these little charmers near bodies of water, where they can gather mud to make their distinctive mud nests on nearby walls, bridges, or even overhangs. While the males are the nest builders in the family and do all the heavy lifting, the females ultimately have the final decision on their mud castles. The Black Phoebe's dusty black cape and hood leave its white belly exposed, making it easy to recognize them after you hear their distinctive "Phoebe" call. Dominating the Flycatcher world, these City Birds do not play well with others and command the air space around their homes. It's a true "no-fly" zone.

BLUE-GRAY GNATCATCHER

···▸ Buggy Brunch, Anyone? ◂···

If you're keeping up with your mental-health walks in the park, be on the lookout for the Blue-gray Gnatcatcher. These bug lovers can be found over a majority of the United States. True to their name, the soft, blue-gray coloring of their feathers and smaller stature make the Blue-gray Gnatcatcher the perfect bug assassin. No need for reservations with the Gnatcatcher—the small invertebrates on their menu are found easily for last-minute dining options. Feasting on spiders, plant bugs, and, of course, gnats, the Gnatcatcher is ruthless, tearing wings off larger prey before devouring the bug body. These City Birds enjoy the wooded areas that city parks provide, because where there are bugs, there are Gnatcatchers. Buildings nests with spiderwebs and lichens, Gnatcatcher parents are attentive and busy. They build several nests in one breeding season, using materials from the old nests. Life in the city is made more pleasurable by the little Gnatcatcher, who helps rid the urban air of pesky flying pests.

BURROWING OWL

···· Basement Apartment Dwellers ····

Located mostly in mid- and central North America, Burrowing Owls can be found in neighborhood yards and arid cities—just look for their burrows. This long-legged ground-dweller earned its name by either building their own burrow or grabbing a fixer-upper from other animals' abandoned burrows. About the size of a Blue Jay, the Burrowing Owl's "resting owl face" gives off quite the serious look, with long eyebrows of feathers forming a stern and serious face. But this species of Owl is more than just a pretty face. The Burrowing Owl is smart enough to put out the welcome mat for yummy bugs by smearing dung along their burrow's entryway, enticing a bevy of insects right to their front door. Picking out dinner just got a lot easier—and no delivery fees!

···› No Scrubs ‹···

The California Scrub Jay graces most West Coast backyards and parks, but these blue-feathered smarties can mainly be found around oak trees—there is no denying their love of a good acorn. Scrub Jays are so stealthy, they'll steal other birds' acorns when those birds are distracted. So, a good rule of thumb is to never turn your back on a California Scrub Jay. Though they aren't very social, these City Birds are extremely smart, and will often hitch a ride on a mule deer in exchange for grazing rights, ridding the deer of ticks and fleas. The California Scrub Jay eats its weight in seeds using its sturdy bill to open those harder nuts to crack. If you hear their high-pitched screech, don't fret—that's just their call. They'll usually announce their arrival at the feeder with an unmistakable squawk, so you'll know when a Scrub Jay has arrived.

···• Tough as (Tiny) Nails •···

The smallest bird in the United States does the most traveling. The Calliope Hummingbird's wanderlust takes them from the northern American states to Central America in a massive migration. These world travelers, as big as a large pecan, will return to favorite perches year after year. Those on the Pacific Coast can catch a glimpse of this emerald-green and pink-throated hummer around flowering plants. The iridescent pink throat feathers are longer than the others, almost like a dazzling beard, giving the Calliope Hummingbird a shine and shimmer that's unique to the hummer family. You'll recognize this City Bird by the buzz of their wings and their squeak-like call. One way to ensure the Calliope visits is to plant the flowers they enjoy. They love tubular flowers, so plant things such as larkspur or bee plants to entice them to your yard. And if they find a bigger bird at the feeder? No problem—the small-but-mighty hummers will simply chase the interlopers away from their favorite foods. Don't mess with the Calliope!

CEDAR WAXWING

···• Party Animals •···

Fruit-loving Cedar Waxwings are a feast for the eyes, and a dream of a farmer's market customer. This striking bird is very distinguished, with crisp feather features, red-tipped wings, and a yellow-tipped tail, as if they were dipped in wax (hence the name). Cedar Waxwings will visit fruit trees and then, like feathered Johnny Appleseeds, deposit digested fruit seeds in their droppings—talk about same-day delivery! Honeysuckle berries are a particular delicacy for Cedar Waxwings, with the added bonus that the berries can change their tipped tail coloring. These City Birds are strict vegetarians; they can also be the life of the party. Believe it or not, the Cedar Waxwing has been known to knock back a few, becoming drunk on fermented seeds. Don't seed and fly!

CERULEAN WARBLER

···• Friendly Neighborhood City Bird •···

Hopping around trees, gobbling up insects, and singing a sweet song, the Cerulean Warbler is not only stunning, but a fun bird to watch. The Cerulean Warbler's blue hues are distinctive and unique in the bird world. This medium-sized City Bird is not difficult to locate—just knowing which trees they frequent (white oaks and maples!) will increase your chances of a sighting on the eastern side of the United States. The best place to find these blue or green birds (male or female, respectively) is a city park. Singing for their supper, these happy birds search an entire tree for their favorite bug supper. Cerulean Warblers commandeer spider webs to use for their nest, building a springy space for their babies to grow. And while most birds fly out of their nest, these City Birds like to live a little more dangerously: they dismount via free fall before taking off into the skies. Eat your heart out, Spider-Man.

···• Tight Squeeze •···

Nimble and bat-like, the Chimney Swift's sooty colors perfectly match the inside of the chimneys they frequent. The Chimney Swift is well adapted to city life, thriving around manmade objects in the eastern and central spaces of North America. These City Birds aren't afraid to get up close and personal, much like their human counterparts on public transit at rush hour. Like a bat, the Chimney Swift clings to tight spaces such as chimneys or tree cavities. Additionally, it spends most of its time in the air foraging for insects, agile enough to catch bugs while in flight. Roosting together at times, Chimney Swifts can be found under overpasses and bridges in their mud houses glued to the walls. It is easy to catch a glimpse of the Chimney Swift in action, but to catch them funneling into their roosting spot like a tornado of birds is quite a sight.

···• Cleared for Takeoff •···

Birdwatchers can't help but feel relaxed as they watch a Common Loon glide gracefully across the water—even amongst the hustle and bustle. In the city, these birds will be found in calmer bodies of water near the shore, often preening themselves for feather care. These waterfowl dive for their dinner, agile enough underwater to compete with the fish. They've also learned to control their release of air as they dive, to stay down longer. Their insatiable appetites and deadly efficiency will quickly deplete a fish population. Common Loons need a runway to fly from the water, which means they must run on top of the water to gain the momentum needed for flight. If you're lucky enough to see a Common Loon, you're sure to be astonished by their elegant appearance and piercing red eyes. Sit back and enjoy the show.

···• Winter Tourists •···

Thriving at the top of the world, the Common Redpoll calls the Arctic home. These small, fluffy birds have a red topknot and a rosy breast, and when they fly south for the winter, they bring the whole family. Flocks in the hundreds travel together, arriving anywhere in the middle of North America when the tundra turns too cold. Meadows are a particular favorite party spot, as the birds search for their favorite nyjer or thistle seeds. Feeders in northern cities will draw in these flying fluff-balls. The Common Redpoll also has no problem with leftovers dropped on the ground, because their small, yellow bills can handle the seed bits. Adapted to cold northern climates, these City Birds will descend upon the city in droves. If there are seeds . . . they will come.

Redpolls have adapted to the cold so well, they've learned how to tunnel in the snow to stay warm.

···• Street Smarts •···

Early American colonists enjoyed the sights and songs of the Common Yellowthroat. This yellow bandit can be found in parks with tangled vegetation and tall grasses, as they prefer bushy fields. The distinctive call of the Common Yellowthroat will lead you to the happy little birds. Don't let appearances deceive you: these City Birds are not only cute, but smart too. Nasty Cowbirds, the most despised amongst birders, will prey on unsuspecting songbirds by leaving an egg in their nests for the parents to raise as their own. The nestling will starve the parents' own offspring and boot them from the nest. (Who among us hasn't had a roommate like that?) But the Common Yellowthroat will abandon the nest if a Cowbird tries to sneak in an egg, ensuring the baby Yellowthroats survive. Once the males have determined the relationship, the females tend to be more . . . *adventurous* in their breeding, which the males seem to tolerate. That's amore!

···• Bottomless Brunch •···

Desert flowers entice the Costa's Hummingbird to live in those arid climates, but once the blooming season ends, they buzz back to the West Coast. Visiting over one thousand plants a day in search of delicious nectar, the Costa's Hummingbird helps keep desert flora in bloom by pollinating the cacti. These Southwest birds will visit flowering shrubs, but the cactus flower is by far their favorite. They're just as pretty as the flowers they visit, with males showing off brilliantly feathered purple hoods. Hummingbird feeders with uncolored sugar water will have them coming back for more, and you may get a chance to see the courtship dances of males swooping and diving while they call out to nearby females.

DARK-EYED JUNCO

···→ Snow Birds ←···

The Dark-eyed Junco is a stylish bird and a trailblazer. While most snowbirds flee to warmer climates for the winter, the Junco is ready for life in the city only once winter hits. Arriving in droves of millions upon millions of birds, when these city-dwellers flock to feeders, take it as a signal that winter has arrived. These fluffy little things are often seen hopping around on the snow, a stunning contrast between the crisp white of the snow and smoky dark feathers of the Junco. A Dark-eyed Junco does *not* do hot. They really don't do warm either—they strictly like the cold. As they constantly forage for seeds, they'll kick up snow as they hunt for treats, gobbling up the seeds dropped by other birds at the feeder. It almost looks like a one-bird snow fight, as they sling snow in search of seeds.

···· Working Hard or Hardly Working ····

About as big as a glass of milk, the Eastern Screech Owl is so well camouflaged, homeowners won't even know their backyard is home to one. For a small owl, it has a big reputation: this Owl's hoot is the infamous one heard in movies. Eastern Screech Owls are year-round residents and offer excellent pest control. Though these City Birds can cause a commotion on the nighttime scene, they enjoy solace and like to sunbathe on cold days. A nesting box and bird bath prove irresistible for these nighttime assassins, so place them in your yard to attract some hooting neighbors. While these birds are monogamous, sometimes the male will have a side chick who may or may not decide to evict the older female. But, when he is dedicated, the male Eastern Screech Owl delivers food for momma and babies, a much-needed reprieve. He's certainly a keeper.

···• Show-stopping Celebirdies •···

Dashing and easy to spot, the Evening Grosbeak is a treat for the eyes, especially when in their exquisite breeding plumage of golden yellows, whites, and blacks. The Evening Grosbeak happily gobbles up buds, berries, and bugs and will never pass up their favorite lunch spot: a maple tree, complete with a menu of bugs drizzled with maple sap. Though they may need to lay off the snacks, as the Grosbeak *is* the heaviest of the Finch family, they can handle foods other birds simply can't. There is no song for this "songbird," but the lack of musical ability is made up for tenfold by the vibrancy of their feathers. This City Bird is sure to stop the show when they arrive on the scene. Since their flight paths are erratic at best, a sighting causes quite a stir among the birding paparazzi. Found at feeders and in trees during the winter, the best way to guarantee a sighting is to search for golden birds in a flock around their favorite dining spots.

···▸ Signature Style ◂···

Snowy white Great Egrets are prevalent throughout the coastal cities of the United States and any space with a water source. These birds are hard to miss as they wade through shallow waters with their long legs and stately stature. (We wonder which modeling agency they've signed with?) Now considered a national treasure, this variety of Egret is "great" indeed. Hunting with fine-tuned precision, the long, lethal bill of the Great Egret hardly misses its intended prey. The Great Egret is an excellent model for amateur photographers aiming to practice their hobby away from the busier parts of the city. If you make waterfront dinner reservations, there is sure to be a sighting.

GREAT HORNED OWL

···› King of the Hill ‹···

One of the most easily recognized birds—and one of the largest in North America—is the Great Horned Owl. With a wingspan the size of a small child, this giant is not gentle, but is in fact quite the predator. Luckily, its diet consists mainly of mice, and not men—though they *can* overtake animals larger than themselves. The Great Horned Owl's yellow eyes do not move, so the distinguished predator will turn its entire head to locate prey. The Great Horned Owl thrives in all landscapes across America, with some people even putting up nesting boxes for the Owls. It's a win/win with this City Bird for a neighbor: they get endless mouse-y snacks and you get excellent pest control. The oldest recorded Great Horned Owl was almost 30 years old, and undoubtedly wise beyond their years.

···• What a Way to Make a Living •···

If you want to get a good look at the Hooded Oriole, it's best to put on your cowboy boots and head West. Sometimes the seasons of change will bring these birds out of their range, but only once a year during migration. Hooded Orioles range in vibrancy from bright yellows to flaming oranges, with black feathering standing in stark contrast. These fine feathered friends also have an extreme sweet tooth. These birds will flock to Hummingbird feeders full of sugar water, even in public spaces.

A surefire way to have these birds as frequent visitors is to put out orange slices—it's an offer they won't refuse. Using their sharp bill to dig into fruits for more delicious nectar, these City Birds just can't get enough. But Hooded Oriole females are no ladies of leisure. They sew together their own nests with leaves and fibers, using their bill as a needle.

···▸ Single and Ready to Mingle ◂···

Introduced to New York in the late 1800s, House Sparrows are both handsome and common. Found throughout the world (except in extremely cold regions), these little birds hop and chirp their way through a variety of landscapes. Attracting these singing immigrants to a feeder is simple enough with bird seed—some people have even been able to hand-feed them. Look for the House Sparrow hopping on the ground and basking in the glorious dust baths they so love. These little sparrows have a pecking order, with older birds fluffing up their extra-speckled neck, hard-earned through years of survival. Nesting in odd spots, stealing food from native birds, and aggressively defending their territory, the House Sparrow isn't likely to be voted a favorite amongst birders. But they fit right in at parks and restaurants across the city. As common little scavengers, they help keep the city clean.

···· Little, but Fierce ····

Located within a small section of the American central west, the adorable Juniper Titmouse can be found hopping, hanging, and harvesting around shrubbery and trees in the Midwest. This small City Bird looks and acts like a tough guy, regardless of its size. The soft gray coloring of their feathers only adds to their cute fierceness. Smart enough to store seeds for the winter, the Juniper Titmouse doesn't leave home once the weather gets cold and will visit backyard feeders while close to the city. Find a juniper tree in a Midwestern city, and if there is a small, gray bird too busy to notice you, it is certainly a Juniper Titmouse.

···· Adventurous Nomads ····

Lewis's Woodpeckers love to snatch tasty insects off trees. Unlike other Woodpeckers who peck their way through dinner, these medium-sized birds use their specialized beak to grab food from the bark of trees they frequent. No forest or tree is off-limits for this Woodpecker's appetite—they'll wander until they find a tasty snack and a place to call home. These City Birds are predominantly located in the western parts of America, though not beyond the Rocky Mountains, and can be identified by their red face, pink chest, and green back. Apt and agile, Lewis's Woodpeckers will perch patiently until a flying insect passes by, and then snatch them right out of the air. Named for none other than one of America's most famous explorers, Meriwether Lewis, this nomadic bird takes after its namesake, always exploring—though in search of nuts or bugs, not necessarily uncharted territories.

···• Green with Envy •···

The distinctive quack of a duck is most likely produced by a nearby female Mallard (the males don't quack). In the city, it's not surprising to find these ducks happy in even the smallest pools of water. After all, as the most common duck in North America, they can be found at basically any water source. Many a city park's lake boasts Mallard pairs smoothly gliding across the calm waters. Spotting the male's emerald-green head means his female is not far away—he can't leave her side, for fear that other males will seek her attention. City Birds move fast! If you live near a body of water, put up a camera near the water's grasses or a planter box close by. Ducks will set up house close to human activity. Once nesting has begun, Mallards shed their flight feathers, making them flightless until the babies are ready to venture out.

Make way for ducklings!

⋯ Rise and Grind ⋯

What's on the menu for the small Merlin Falcon? Definitely bird. Positioned at the highest points, atop trees or light poles, the Merlin will snatch and devour other birds in an instant. Easily adaptable, the Merlin has learned to live in populous places, taking advantage of manmade structures to gain helpful vantage points. They'll catch unsuspecting birds in flight or swoop down upon them on the ground with deadly accuracy. If everyone in the city was as patient as a Merlin, the city would slow to a pace where not much is accomplished in a day but one thing: dinner. These birds will freeze, patiently waiting for their prey until the precise moment arrives to strike. Strike first, and strike hard—this is the Merlin's mantra for City Bird life. Search tall structures for a glimpse of this speed demon, because their pursuits are almost too fast to catch a glimpse.

MUTE SWAN

···· Delete the Dating Apps ····

A symbol of enduring love and dedication, the Mute Swan mates for life. Though Swans can be found in abundance on lakes within city parks, these birds are not actually native to America, but have adapted and thrived. Mute Swans dine on aquatic vegetation, devouring essential hiding spots and food for others. Though graceful, perhaps they aren't the best neighbors! Nesting pairs build works of art with massive reed nests more like a floating palace for bird royalty than a stick nest found in trees. When observing the Muted Swan in the wild, do not trespass in their territory, because they will aggressively defend their water turf. And while Mute Swans are beauty in motion, they are even more thrilling when spotted out on the town with the whole family.

··· Accomplished Architects ···

A towering nest, a great architectural feat that defies gravity, is home to one of America's more impressive birds, the Osprey. You can easily spot their massive nests, which are more likely to be on the outskirts of the city near water. Don't we all find ourselves longing for a home in the suburbs? But Ospreys have been known to build nests within the city limits on tall structures, as long as the city is near a shoreline, as these predators are pescatarians. The Osprey is deserving of much respect and admiration, soaring high above others and capable of crossing the continent in one massive trek—with some breaks, of course. When this bird decides to pack up and leave, it travels far for its new hunting ground. People often confuse an Osprey with a Bald Eagle, but the white eye stripe and softer white coloring of the Osprey are quite different from the bold, all-white feather top of the Bald Eagle. The only raptor to dive headfirst in a deep dive for fish, the Osprey will out-fish even the best fisherman—talk about catch of the day.

···· Southern Charm ····

Typically a southern bird, the Painted Bunting is one of America's most beautiful birds. So beautiful, in fact, they look painted—hence the name. The vivid reds, blues, and yellows of their feathers makes them picture perfect. Yet beneath all that beauty, these City Birds are relatively low maintenance. While they love seeds, they are just as happy to grab insects for a quick meal. If you spot a Bunting in a park, know that the males are territorial, keeping acres of land all for themselves. Native grasses and gardens are best to bring in these hungry birds. These birds have specialty nests, woven from grasses in the trees. The best chance to observe these dazzling beauties is to search their favorite spaces for food and keep a sharp eye out at the edges of city and country. You might get to enjoy the flying art show before they head to Central America and the Caribbean for the winter.

···• Fast and Furious •···

Making great use of ledges and bridges to nest in cities, the Peregrine Falcon takes what it wants. This elite predator is fast and furious when hunting for supper, with any bird on the menu. This Falcon, like others in its family, feasts on medium-sized birds, often diving from great heights to capture a meal. The Peregrine Falcon takes the title of fastest animal on the planet while in its pursuit dive. Found in most of North America, search high-rise ledges for this beautiful City Bird. The Peregrine Falcon is probably the most impressive Falcon on the North American continent. But it isn't all fast flying. Humans enjoy watching the Peregrine's tender care of its white, fluffy chicks too (on livestream, of course—keep your distance!). Peregrine Falcons will nest in an artificial box on a building, so consider installing one (after the necessary approvals) and be sure to add a camera to allow your neighbors the chance to follow along.

PINE SISKIN

···• A Sunny Disposition •···

The Pine Siskin is aptly named, based on their love of conifers. This little bird likes to hang on branches—often upside down—to find and devour seeds at every opportunity. Their love of sunflower seeds will keep them coming back to manmade feeders for seconds, and they often drag their best friends, the Goldfinches, along for the ride. The Pine Siskin offers a nice pop of color when they show up for a winter feeding, but the problem is no one can really depend on their migratory patterns. The birds flock to the seeds of the trees, so one year the birds may be plentiful and the next, they are a no-show. These nomads of the sky can show up anywhere, at any time, in the lower 48 states.

···· Dark Wings Take to Flight ····

The Raven, well known for dressing in all black—even down to the eyes—like any good city-dweller, is one of the smartest birds in the feathered world. Their high intelligence is often overlooked because they are also the greasers of the community, but these shaggy, scrappy birds have been known to use tools to get their food. Some of the most famous Ravens even call the Tower of London home, while others storm the stadium on Sundays to show off their Baltimore pride. Strutting around, exuding confidence, the Raven thrives around communities due to its adaptability and ability to mimic manmade sounds. They use their remarkable skills to recall faces and return to familiar stomping grounds. They're also known to hold a grudge against any bird or person who has betrayed them. Immortalized by Edgar Allan Poe (who has three major cities—Baltimore, Philadelphia, and Boston—fighting to call him their hometown macabre hero), the Raven is a romantic—and spooky—resident of any city, blending right in with the cosmopolitan crowd.

···· Real Estate Moguls ····

The Red-bellied Woodpecker does have a red belly—we promise—it's just not easily spied unless the bird is positioned perfectly. Like all Woodpeckers, the red-bellied version has the quintessential sharp beak for pecking and the elongated tongue for bug retrieval. In the bird world, it's that tongue of theirs that's truly unique. For one, underneath the beautiful feathers, the tongue is so long it quite literally wraps around this City Bird's skull, finding its resting place in a groove at the top of the head. Using their tongue like a whip, the Red-bellied Woodpecker snags bugs in an instant. Hummingbird feeders will attract Red-bellied Woodpeckers, because their tongues can lap up the sweet nectar found within, though hammering bugs out of dead trees is, of course, their favorite dining option. Once it's time to settle down, the Red-bellied Woodpecker crafts a cozy home, but they have to be vigilant to pay the rent on time because their nesting cavity is a hot commodity. It's all fun and games until the Starling shows up to steal your home—there goes the neighborhood!

···• I'm Walking Here! •···

There is no visit to a city without a Rock Pigeon sighting. Common and calm, these City Birds are so accustomed to people they're almost a nuisance. Opportunists for a quick meal, they waste no time gobbling up whatever they find on the streets of the city—they aren't choosy. Be careful where you sit in a public city space, as these birds can mess up a park bench quicker than a crosswalk countdown, and keep your eyes open as you walk down the sidewalk to make sure you don't trip over this fearless feathered friend. Historically, Rock Pigeons were vital during the First and Second World Wars, carrying messages for the military. Even further back, this humble Pigeon even played a role in Charles Darwin's theory of evolution. These City Birds will nest on buildings and window ledges close to their food source, whether that's a park, restaurant, or feeder. If it's quick and easy, it's their favorite.

SAVANNAH SPARROW

···• No Place Like Home •···

As most city-dwellers know, there is beauty in the ordinary, and that is certainly the case with the adorable Savannah Sparrow. This songbird is found all over the North American continent in great numbers. Thriving in the city, people find themselves smiling just watching the Savannah Sparrow hop around on sidewalks and pecking at patrons' crumbs as their main course. The hardest worker in the family is the mother, who feeds not only the brood, but also herself. She's a tough little lady and doesn't need a man to take care of her. She also gets a little more rest than other new moms, because Sparrow babies grow up fast—literally. They are ready to spread their wings and fly the nest in just eight short days. The most endearing part of the Savannah Sparrow's story is their appreciation for home, as they always come back to where they were hatched.

···· Strictly Vegetarians ····

Onlookers can barely believe their eyes when a flock of white Snow Geese takes to the sky. The mesmerizing show of hundreds upon hundreds of birds can be viewed by simply looking up from any vantage point in North America when a flock is on the move. Snow Geese will travel from the crisp climate of the Canadian tundra to the warmer Southern United States for the winter. (Admit it—you're jealous.) City residents will enjoy these birds while they are in flight and can follow them to the closest flooded field. There, Snow Geese will forage for food. People are often unprepared for the size of the flock and the noise these chatty birds make. There is a variant of Snow Goose that is a darker color, called the blue morph. These darker birds can be found dotted within the pearly flock, like polka-dots in the sky or field.

···• The Next Big Thing •···

The Steller's Jay's resume is quite impressive. They boast beauty, brains, and a talent for mimicry! With gorgeous, deep cerulean blues and shades of charcoal grays, the Steller's Jay is a showstopper, turning heads on any city sidewalk. This western bird loves evergreen trees, bird feeders, and picnic tables, so the best place to find this Jay is a public park. Known for stealing picnic food (sometimes right out of a human's hand), the large Steller's Jay is not to be trifled with. They're unaffected by the presence of people and quite territorial around other birds. If you hear a cat's mew or a squirrel's bark in a city park, that may actually be a Steller's Jay—they have quite the mimic range.

···• Work Smarter, Not Harder •···

A sophisticated and formal bird, the Tricolored Heron was once known as the Louisiana Heron, but they're actually found in waters along America's coasts. Though they are a tiny replica of a Great Blue Heron, the Tricolored is a beauty in its own right, with feathers in shades of blue and a distinctive white stripe down its chest. Since different members of the Heron family enjoy hanging out together, that white stripe is the best way to identify the Tricolored version. The majority of these birds frequent the shallow waters along US coastal cities from Corpus Christi, TX, to Boston, MA. Look for the Tricolored silently stalking its prey, almost a graceful dance of death, for any creature on their menu. The Tricolored Heron will shadow other fishing birds and then quickly nab the fish as they surface before anyone else can.

···· Why Buy When You Can Thrift? ····

The Tufted Titmouse is as cute as they come, with its spiky little hair feathers and soft gray body. Most likely to be found at a feeder in the city, these little birds will become a regular anywhere with sunflower seeds. Always prepared, the Tufted Titmouse will hoard shelled seeds and stash them away in their nesting cavity for winter. The Titmouse is also a thrifty City Bird, not minding a quick move-in at the former residence of a Woodpecker. And do they have an eye for design! They decorate their new homes with animal hair found out and about. If you want to attract these beauties, put up feeders and leave any dead trees nearby, as both provide the food and shelter they seek. Scattering animal clippings after a trip to doggie daycare will help the Titmouse feather its nest. These birds know how to repurpose and reuse!

⋯• Clean-up Crew •⋯

The Turkey Vulture keeps the planet free of dead debris by eating carrion. When you see these birds circling in the sky just outside the city limits, it's a good bet some unfortunate animal met its demise. The easiest way to tell a Turkey Vulture in flight is to look for the rickracked feathers on the edges of the wings. And while these scavengers often eat human leftovers, the Turkey Vulture's favorite delicacy is dead meat. They can locate the dead and dying from just one whiff on the wind. Always remember, Turkey Vultures are best viewed from afar. They *will* projectile-vomit deceased matter onto your person when threatened. They also have a nasty habit of sticking their feet in animal waste to cool off. It's a dirty job, but somebody's got to do it.

VARIED THRUSH

Hopping around on freshly watered green space, the Varied Thrush happily hunts worms from Alaska to Baja, California. Often spotted with Robins, the Varied Thrush has more brilliant coloring, with a distinct flame-orange traveling to its head and wings as opposed to the red of the Robin's breast. To attract this beauty, plant native fruit and nut shrubbery, as these birds find it hard to resist their favorite foods (second only to worms). Since it belongs to the Thrush family, this bird is mainly a ground feeder and finds comfort in the lower portion of its environment. Just because heights aren't their favorite doesn't mean they won't do what is necessary to defend their territory. Varied Thrushes can be quite domineering, commanding attention from other birds when they are on the scene. Look for them throwing up leaf litter searching for juicy worms or with their friends the Robins.

···• World Travelers •···

Even though the White-throated Sparrow breeds, sings, and spends most of its time in Canada, these birds have dual citizenship, enjoying America's southern climates during the winter. You'll be hard-pressed to find a more cosmopolitan bird than this frequent flyer! Attracting White-throated Sparrows is easy enough: build a brush pile, place a feeder nearby, and watch these songbirds in action. Birders can easily recognize them by the distinctive cadence of their "Oh, Sweet, Canada, Canada" song. If that isn't enough, while in the field their white throats and yellow eyebrows will ensure identification. Females choose their mate based on preferences in coloring patterns, finding males with an opposite color pattern to themselves as most attractive. Opposites truly attract here.

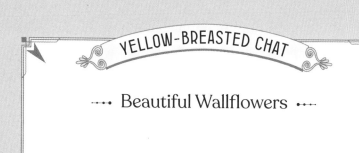

YELLOW-BREASTED CHAT

···• Beautiful Wallflowers •···

Shy Yellow-breasted Chats brighten any day when they appear on the scene. Hidden in underbrush at the forest's edge, these blissful birds seek safety along city park trails. Wallflowers by nature, Yellow-breasted Chats don't know their own beauty. They're happy to blend into the background, singing their repertoire of songs from whistles to chirps to cheeps. The ladies keep the fellas in check, often disapproving of aggressive behavior. Once they nest, these City Birds sadly can't tell the difference between their own precious cargo and those of the Cowbird, often raising the Cowbird baby as their own and displacing their own young. These introverted birds may not be the most flashy, but they're still fun to watch and their song is quite delightful.

YELLOW-RUMPED WARBLER

···• Showing Off Their Assets •···

Migrating in large flocks, Yellow-rumped Warblers can be identified by the flash of yellow on their tiny rumps. Showing up all around town, these adorable little birds sing, flock, and feed communally with their feathered friends. Sometimes you'll find them in the treetops, other times at backyard feeders. They'll show up in droves for those crafty peanut-butter pine cones rolled in seeds. Delighting the young and old alike—and affectionally known as "butter butts"—these Warblers, like any good urbanite, enjoy dining al fresco. The Yellow-rumped Warbler is able to digest more difficult seeds than their Warbler relatives, so they can travel farther north and have the table to themselves. Surviving tough winters doesn't pose a problem for the Yellow-rumped Warbler, since they are versatile foragers, dining on bugs and berries. These City Birds think highly of themselves, often showing dominance over other Warbler species. Who are we to argue?

Out on the
Town

Finding City Birds can be as simple as a walk in the park.

Though the bright lights and busy life of the city keep people moving, everyone needs some down time. Birding offers a budget-friendly chance for introverts and extroverts alike to de-stress, and the opportunity to become an advocate for conservation by calling for the protection of necessary habitats for our feathered friends. The birds have adapted to human life, often thriving around cities and finding their niche within the ecosystem, but we can help them out too.

The beauty of birding is that almost anyone can wake up one day and decide to become a birder. Not many hobbies have such an easy introduction. Start small by simply sitting and observing and learning the frequent flyers in your neighborhood, and then upgrade to a field guide or app for identification. Keep track of the birds you see using the journal pages at the back of this book. Make note of funny characteristics and your unique observations. Even the smallest of birds has a big personality! If nothing else, birding will help you clear your mind and find peace—all good things in a busy, busy world.

Washington

Oregon

Montana

North Dakota

South Dakota

Wyoming

Idaho

Nevada

Nebraska

Utah

Colorado

Kansas

California

Oklahom

Arizona

New Mexico

Texas

Alaska

1	Acorn Woodpecker	11	Blue-gray Gnatcat
2	American Kestrel	12	Burrowing Owl
3	Anna's Hummingbird	13	California Scrub Ja
4	Bald Eagle	14	Calliope Humming
5	Band-tailed Pigeon	15	Cedar Waxwing
6	Belted Kingfisher	16	Cerulean Warbler
7	Bewick's Wren	17	Chimney Swift
8	Black-billed Magpie	18	Common Loon
9	Black-crowned Night Heron	19	Common Redpoll
10	Black Phoebe	20	Common Yellowthr

These Streets Will Make You Feel Brand New

···• The Geography of City Birds •···

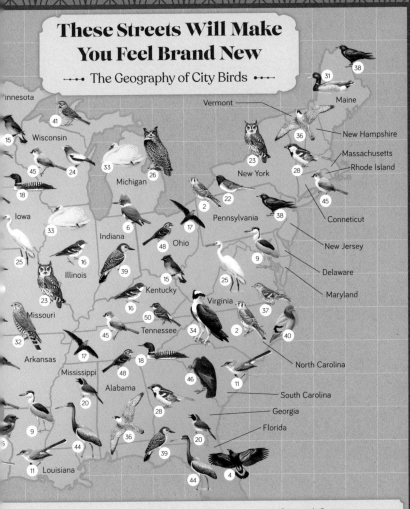

21 Costa's Hummingbird	31 Mallard	41 Savannah Sparrow
22 Dark-eyed Junco	32 Merlin	42 Snow Goose
23 Eastern Screech Owl	33 Mute Swan	43 Steller's Jay
24 Evening Grosbeak	34 Osprey	44 Tricolored Heron
25 Great Egret	35 Painted Bunting	45 Tufted Titmouse
26 Great Horned Owl	36 Peregrine Falcon	46 Turkey Vulture
27 Hooded Oriole	37 Pine Siskin	47 Varied Thrush
28 House Sparrow	38 Raven	48 White-throated Sparrow
29 Juniper Titmouse	39 Red-bellied Woodpecker	49 Yellow-breasted Chat
30 Lewis's Woodpecker	40 Rock Pigeon	50 Yellow-rumped Warbler

Walking the Walk

Every place on Earth has its own set of unspoken rules, and nowhere is that more apparent than in urban centers. Whether you're a lifelong city resident or making the big move for the first time, here are some helpful city dos and don'ts to keep you moving.

•—•—•—•—•—•

DO walk when you can: Walking in the city is often faster than trying to drive or catch a ride. Get in those steps—and those precious birding moments!

DO make time for good meals: You have to eat anyway, so why not make the most of your meal times by strengthening city connections? Business lunches are a time-honored city tradition, and a long, bottomless Sunday brunch with friends will give you time to catch up and decompress.

DO have a great audiobook or podcast downloaded and ready to go: Facing a long subway commute or an hour in rush-hour traffic? Audiobooks and podcasts will make the time fly. Public libraries will let you borrow audiobooks for free and there are podcasts available on everything from pop culture to hard science. Time management is essential to city life— this allows you to multitask!

DO embrace the city's varied cultural offerings: Taste foods from other countries, visit museum exhibitions, and take in a show to immerse yourself in another world. True personal growth comes with learning about others and their culture.

DO give back: Common courtesy can often be pushed aside when in a hurry, but simple acts of kindness can improve someone's day. Allow someone to go ahead of you on the metro, hold the elevator or a door open, or even purchase a quick meal for someone who needs it, if you have the means.

— • — • — ● — • — • —

DON'T get stuck behind a slowpoke: Whether you're late for a meeting or just appreciate a quick pace, politely steer around slower walkers. You've got places to be!

DON'T be caught without a place to sit: It's a sad day if the only seat available is covered in bird droppings (or another mystery substance). Always carry some cleaning wipes in your bag to clean up a spot to sit—just in case.

DON'T travel at rush hour (if you can avoid it!): Entering the city is like going to the amusement park—traveling at strategic hours for work or other obligations will save you time.

DON'T go to a restaurant unprepared: Whether you're trying to impress your boss at lunch or seem sophisticated on a first date, look up the restaurant ahead of time so you have an idea of what the menu looks like.

DON'T stay away from the tourist traps: Be a tourist in your own city! Take the bus tour, visit the major historical sites, and try the ridiculous chain restaurant in that busy part of town. There is so much to learn, see, and do in the city, and you should enjoy it all. Then you can also make good recommendations when family and friends come to visit.

Be a Part of It

When you spot a fascinating bird on the sidewalk or in a city park, make note of the sighting on these pages!

Type of Bird

Date | Location

Notes

Type of Bird

Date | Location

Notes

Type of Bird

Date | Location

Notes

Type of Bird

Date | Location

Notes

Type of Bird

Date | Location

Notes

Type of Bird

Date | Location

Notes

Type of Bird

Date | Location

Notes

Type of Bird

Date | Location

Notes

Type of Bird

Date | Location

Notes

Type of Bird

Date | Location

Notes

Type of Bird

Date | Location

Notes

Type of Bird

Date | Location

Notes

Type of Bird

Date | Location

Notes

Type of Bird

Date | Location

Notes

Type of Bird

Date | Location

Notes

125

Type of Bird

Date | Location

Notes

Type of Bird

Date | Location

Notes

Type of Bird

Date | Location

Notes

Type of Bird

Date | Location

Notes

Women of Letters

Angela Harrison Vinet and **Janis Hatten Harrison**
are a mother/daughter duo who have been writing
these bird books during Janis's battle with bone cancer.
They have found great joy amid darkness while
working together on this series. The perfect pair,
Janis is the birding expert and comic relief while
Angela is the writer and teacher at heart.

Top of the Heap

I would like to thank the Guide to North American Birds and the Cornell Labs' All About Birds websites for creating free, easy-to-use resources. Educating the public about habitat conservation not only protects the animals that live within that space, but also those that pass through. Our world is built upon connections, to one another, to animals, and to the environments we share. Time spent in nature heals us in mind, body, and spirit. When we neglect our environment, we are essentially neglecting ourselves.

I would also like to acknowledge the Indigenous peoples of America, who lived upon the land long before it was America.

—Angela

•–•–•–**•**–•–•–•

A final note to memorialize Flaco the Owl, a king among City Birds, who flew free through New York City for a year and captured the hearts of city-dwellers everywhere.